S... work
-Why Not?

Daphne J Ashby
& Jackie Woolsey

Jackie Woolsey

January 2001

DEDICATION

We would like to dedicate this book to
Bea, Liz and Allison at "Classic Stitches" magazine
who first really stimulated our interest in stumpwork

We would also like to express our grateful thanks to Jill Kempster
(Jackie's sister) for her meticulous proof-checking,
without which the text would have contained many disasters!

Other books by the same authors:

Ribbon Embroidery
> published by David & Charles, Newton Abbott
> Hardback - September 1996, Paperback - August 1998

Creative Embroidery Techniques using Colour through Gold
> published by the Guild of Master Craftsman Publications
> Lewes - June 1998

Why not make a Beaded Amulet Purse?
> self-published - June1998

Why not Carry on Beading?
> self-published - June 1999

Why not make a Box? (by Jackie)
> self-published - September 1996

Making Hand-Sewn Boxes (by Jackie)
> published by the Guild of Master Craftsman Publications
> Lewes - April 1999

This book first published in the UK in January 2001
by Daphne J Ashby & Jackie Woolsey
The Firs, Burgh St Peter, Beccles NR34 0BU
email: jackiewoolsey@talk21.com

ISBN 0-9540030-0-4

Contents

Details taken from a piece of 17th century raised embroidery in the collection of the Norfolk Museums & Archaeology Service and held at The Costume & Textile Study Centre, Carrow House, Norwich, to whom we are grateful for permission to reproduce these photographs.

STUMPWORK - A few background notes

History

Stumpwork was at the height of its popularity during the 17th century. This was the age of oak, when rooms had heavily panelled walls and oak beams, and the use of fabric became important. It is therefore not surprising that this heavy three-dimensional type of embroidery became popular.

It has had other names, sometimes being called raised, embossed or even embosted embroidery. It was mainly used as a covering for boxes and caskets, and for panels, mirror surrounds, cushions and book covers. Vibrant colours were used, often on white silk satin. Work has been discovered unfinished, revealing that they worked using a black outline on the white fabric and it is thought that kits were sold with the outline of the embroidery clearly marked. Girls as young as 11 to 14 were often taught and some of their work was named and included their ages.

Surviving historical items include:

1. Needle-made fabrics called needlelace.
2. Wires and vellum bound with thread.
3. Amongst items used as embellishment are pearls, beads, semi-precious stones, real hair, feathers, mica, metal threads, braid, purl and fragments of woven tapestry.
4. Miniature designs with minute details.
5. Strong use of figurative subjects within a natural background.

Prior to stumpwork becoming popular, padded figures were often used, especially in ecclesiastical pieces, and needlelace was often found in Elizabethan embroidery.

An unusual aspect of this type of work is that no scale was involved; insects were often as large as animals, flowers as big as castles and the moon and sun often appear together on a single piece.

Most designs included a fountain, fish, castle or country mansion, costumed figures, animals, the sun, clouds and the moon.

Popular themes included:

1. Biblical stories
2. Incidents from myths and legends
3. Allegorical themes including the four seasons, the four elements earth, air, fire and water, the senses and the virtues.
4. Single figures and groups, Kings and Queens, and ladies and gentlemen with their retainers.
5. Commemorative events; these were often dated with the date when it was worked rather than the date when the event took place.

Materials and Equipment

Fabric

Traditionally, this type of work was always carried out on thick, white, silk satin which was imported from Italy.

Modern work can use any background fabric but finer fabrics should always be backed with a firm cotton to make it strong enough to support the weight of the embroidery.   Calico is also needed on which to work any detached elements.

Pelmet Vilene is useful as backing.

Threads

A wide variety of threads can be used in stumpwork, from the finest to the thickest.

Stranded cotton or silk used down to just a single thread.   Experiment with variegated threads to give shading where it is difficult to keep changing your thread, such as in needlelace.

Cotton perle is ideal for weaving.

Thicker threads, such as soft cotton, are useful for padding and wrapping.

Use the velvet texture of such threads as chenille for special effects, such as a hairy caterpillar body.

Rayon machine embroidery threads, which are fine and shiny, are ideal for any fine details such as insects legs, spiders webs and outlining. These threads are also available with the addition of a metallic element which can enhance the work.

Invisible nylon thread can be very useful for adding beads, sequins, leather, etc.

Needles

A selection of needles are essential for stumpwork because of the different types of thread in use. Be sure that the needles you are using are large enough not to spoil the thread, yet will not make too large a hole in the fabric. A double thread should be able to pass through the fabric reasonably easily.

You will also need a large-eyed darning needle to make a hole in the fabric to put the wires through. (You may even need a stiletto.) A curved needle too would be helpful for attaching shapes already embroidered.

A blunt tapestry needle is essential for weaving threads, working woven stitches and making needlelace; this will help avoid splitting the threads.

Frames

Stumpwork should always be worked with the background fabric stretched tightly, either on a rectangular wooden frame or on a circular wooden hoop.

If a circular hoop is used, ensure that the inner ring is bound with cotton tape. (A cheap tape is good because it is slightly less bulky than a good quality one.) Be especially careful if you are mounting a backed fabric into a hoop: make sure each fabric is stretched tightly. Remember a small scrap of precious fabric can be stitched onto a piece of cotton (the back of which is cut away before embroidering) if it is not large enough to fit your frame.

If a rectangular frame is used, staple the fabric onto it or use drawing pins. If drawing pins are used, cover the heads with masking tape to ensure that the threads do not catch on them.

Stumpworkers need to hoard all kinds of treasures, from tiny beads and sequins through to small scraps of leather and fragments of old lace and ribbon.

Wires

Cake wires can be used to shape detached petals and leaves, etc. Covered wires have a thin layer of paper wrapped tightly round them. Size 28 or 30 can be used for leaves or petals. These can be bent easily and obtained in several colours, including green and white. Use an old pair of scissors or wire cutters for cutting the wires - good scissors can easily be spoiled.

It is a good idea to have some uncovered wires, e.g. fine florist wire or thick fuse wire, as these are useful to outline insect wings and make feelers.

Fray Check

This is a liquid which dries to become invisible and is used when cutting an edge of fabric that may fray if untreated. There are several different makes and instructions about drying time, etc., may vary, so please read the instructions carefully.

Bondaweb

Bondaweb (paper with a glue backing sold from a roll) will fuse two fabrics together so is useful if you are working on a background and wish to add a motif from another fabric. Again there are several makes on the market and instructions will vary.

Other equipment

Finely pointed embroidery scissors
Pins
Thimble
Tweezers for handling small items.

Stumpwork - General Instructions

Padding with felt

To form a raised area, trace the desired shape and cut out. Cut two or three more shapes, decreasing each one in size. For example, if you were padding a flower centre, the following circular shapes would be used:

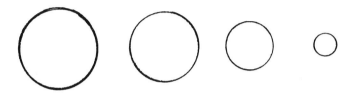

Cut the resulting shapes out in felt. At this stage, you can, if you wish, embroider the largest shape. It is quite a good idea to back this largest shape with Vilene to give a better surface on which to embroider.

Start to apply the shapes over the area to be raised with the smallest shape. Stitch this all round by coming up by the side of the shape and going down into the felt. Apply each layer directly over the previous one and stitch as before. If you have already embroidered the top layer, make your stitches form part of the embroidery.

If you have not embroidered the top shape, once it is in place, you can satin stitch over it, starting in the centre of the shape and working to the sides, thus avoiding the stitches "falling off".

Wiring a shape to be cut out

Stretch a piece of calico on a round frame. Draw the shape onto the right side of the fabric. Lay a length of wire around the shape and couch into place. Blanket stitch over the wire, using small neat stitches lying close to each other.

If the shape is to be a petal, the ends of the wire will be left free, so that they can be put through the fabric when attaching the petal to the flower.

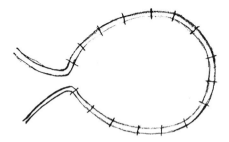

If the shape is to be a leaf, lay a length of wire up the central vein, leaving an end of wire about 1" long where the stem would be. Couch up the vein and put two stitches at the top, bend the wire to go down one side of the leaf and couch until you get to the bottom of the leaf and then bend to go up the other side, stopping about ½" from the top. Cut the wire about ¾" from where the last stitch will be. Push the wire through the fabric and continue to couch the wire on. When you reach the top, turn the work over and secure the end of the wire along the back of the central vein. Now blanket stitch over the couched wire, using tiny, neat stitches.

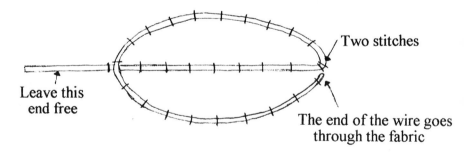

Two stitches

Leave this
end free

The end of the wire goes
through the fabric

Work round the shape with long and short stitch, each stitch coming up inside the shape and going down inside the loop made by the blanket stitch.

Continue to work the remainder of the shape in long and short stitch, shading the colours.

There are so many lovely printed fabrics available which can be used in stumpwork.

A section of the fabric can be stretched into a circular frame and flower petals, leaves or even insects can be worked in this way and then cut out and added to a piece of work.   A blanket stitch edge and one row at least of long and short stitch will have to be worked.

<u>Needlelace shapes</u>

For these shapes you will need a piece of stiff plastic sheet to work over. (The sort of plastic folder used for holding papers and which is fairly strong will be suitable for this purpose.) With a brightly coloured thread, couch a wire to the shape required onto the plastic sheet with stitches about 1 cm apart. Then with the correctly coloured thread, blanket stitch round the wire (<u>not</u> through the plastic), this time with the loop of the blanket stitch on the inside of the shape.

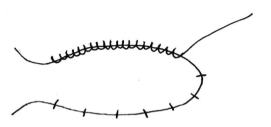

The filling detached blanket stitch is then worked into the loops of the blanket stitches of the previous row. This can be done by working round the shape or by filling in with rows of blanket stitch. If rows are worked, do the first row into the loops and then each other row will be worked into the preceding row of loops, going into the stitches at each end of the row.

Remove the leaf from the plastic backing by carefully cutting the brightly coloured threads.

Leaves in Stumpwork

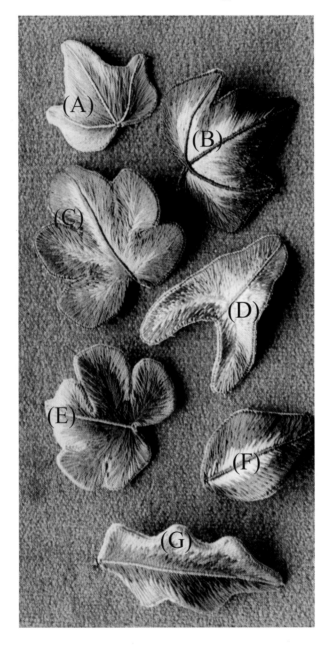

LEAVES IN STUMPWORK

Wired and shaded leaves

There are many different shaped leaves and the examples here have all been worked with single threads. This makes it far easier to get an even result when shading with long and short stitches. It is very important to keep your stitching at a sharp angle to the main vein.

If you have difficulty keeping at the sharp angle, just draw in a few straight lines in pencil to help you.

Looking at the photograph on the previous page, the threads used for the leaves are:

(A) Fine silk   (E) Flower thread
(B) Indian rayon   (F) Coton a broder
(C) Six strand cotton   (G) Coton Perle No. 8
(D) Marlitt

These are in order of thickness, starting with the finest.

Both (A) and (B) are ivy leaves and you will see they look very different as the first one starts with the palest thread outside and the second one has a very dark edge and gets paler towards the centre of the leaf. Remember too that some leaves have patches of colour rather than even shading. A good example of this is the shrub Eleagnus (a favourite with flower arrangers) or a Coleus plant.

The two ivy leaves have a central vein plus one on either side this makes the leaf more flexible. For a palmatic shaped leaf (handshaped) you may need a wire for each section of the leaf.

14

For the more simple shaped leaves, the wiring is started with a short stem, which remains unattached, then goes up the central vein, down the left hand side of the leaf and back up the right hand side. The second end of the wire goes through the fabric at the top of the leaf and a short end of about ½" is folded behind the central vein and stitched in place.

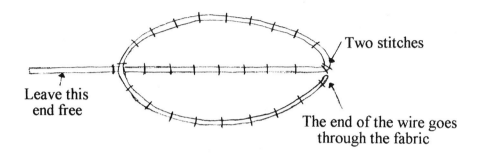

Two stitches

Leave this
end free

The end of the wire goes
through the fabric

The wire for the central vein should be slightly curved to look more natural.

With the ivy leaf, a second wire is used, starting at A and ending at B. Both ends were put through the fabric and caught down behind the vein.

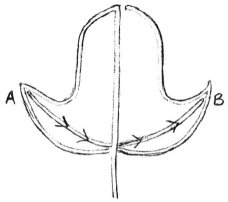

Remember too that leaves can be quite colourful, for example, the geranium named Mrs Henry Cox, which is mainly grown for its foliage rather than the flowers.

Always, when wishing to re-create the realism of nature, the more shades of colour you use the better will be the effect. Five different shades of green were used in the first ivy leaf (A), shown top left in the photograph at the beginning of this section.

If you intend to curl the edge of the leaf over, remember the back, as your work will have to look as good there as on the front!

Woven leaves

Initially, it is necessary to create the skeleton of the leaf from wire and this is then worked in the hand. Following the diagrams, fold the wire in half (if you are making a leaf that is 1" in length, start with a piece of wire 7" long) and then fold the wire back on itself with the ends extending beyond the leaf to make the stalk for fixing it to the embroidery.

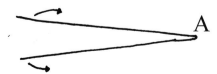

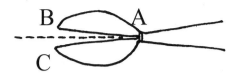

Join a thread on at A leaving the loose end up behind the wires, as shown by the dotted line. Take the thread up to the point of the leaf and stitch together points B & C. You are now ready to start weaving. Remember to hold the side wires out to keep the leaf shapes.

If a group of leaves is needed, bind the stem of the first leaf for about ½" and put to one side. Work a second leaf in the same way and then bind the two stems together. Continue in this way until the required number of leaves have been assembled.

Examples of greetings cards which can provide inspiration for
stumpwork flowers - see Suppliers' List for details

Flowers in Stumpwork

Before you start to embroider flowers in stumpwork, look carefully to see the arrangement of the petals - the back petals (those furthest away) can be stitched onto the background fabric and then gradually work forward.

Do the petals overlap? Are the edges folded over? If they are folded, are they turned away from you or towards you? Are they a different colour underneath? Are the petals darker on the outside or in the centre?

These are all questions that need to be answered before you begin to stitch.

Next, you have to find either a real flower and dissect the petals to see the shape when they are flat, or a good photograph from which you can imagine what happens and draw them. Trace your petals and number them in the order in which they will be added.

Look at your flower centre - how will you work this? French knots or beads could be used or a mixture of both? Remember, with natural subjects, the more colours used the better will be the results.

There are several ways that flowers can be worked:

1. Petals that are wired and shaded - poppies, single roses, iris, etc.
2. Petals made with needlelace.
3. Flowers formed with beads - grape hyacinths.
4. Flowers made with ribbon loops - dandelions, daisies, etc.
5. Flowers with raised centres to be padded with felt - daisies, heleniums, etc.

The projects that follow are examples of using some of the above ideas.

Pansy

The pansy has five petals and here the back two are worked onto the background fabric. The two side petals, 3 and 4, are added next and, finally, 5 sits in front of the others. The pansy was worked in flower thread.

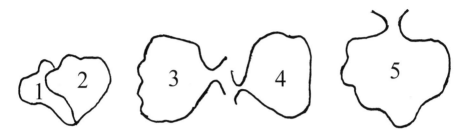

Poppy

A poppy has just four petals. The two side petals, 1 and 2, are attached first, followed by the top petal, no. 3, and finally the lower petal, no. 4. The centre is raised over a circle of felt and is stitched in pale green and dark navy. (See photograph.) Finally the stamens are stitched using dark navy thread and tiny black beads. Remember that the stitches need to be irregular in length. The outer stitching was worked with flower thread and the remainder in Madeira Rayon No. 40.

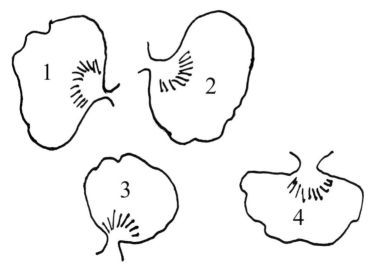

Nasturtium

The nasturtium has five petals and the top two have more depth of colour than the others and these are wired and stitched on as Nos. 1 and 2. (None of the petals are stitched on the background.) The outside stitching is in flower thread and the remainder in Indian rayon thread.

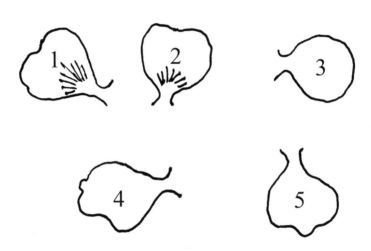

Poinsettia

For this flower, a printed fabric was used, from which a flower was cut out as a base. Bondaweb was applied and the flower cut out and sealed to the background fabric using a hot iron. The outline was then stitched as close to the flower edge as possible with a chain stitch in gold thread. Again using the printed fabric, the five top petals were wired, blanket-stitched in gold and then just one row of stitching was worked around them in red and a centre vein added in gold. These were then cut out and applied and a centre of beads added.

24

Fuchsia

The stem, body and petals 1 and 2 are worked directly onto the background fabric. Next use long stitches to form the stamens - see photograph opposite - positioning a bead at the ends. Then petals 3 and 4 are wired, stitched and then placed in position, forming a "skirt" over petals 1 and 2. The upstanding petals are then wired, stitched and added - nos. 5, 6 and 7.

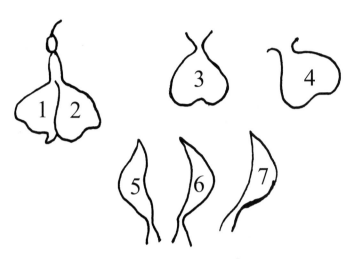

Iris

The stem, sepals and petals 1, 2 and 3 are stitched directly onto the background fabric, leaving a space between the sepals and petals, as indicated in the diagram. The side petals, 4 and 5, are added next and, finally, petal 6 lays over the front. These are all worked using the wiring method.

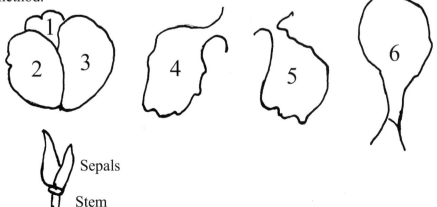

Magnolia

The first six of the magnolia's petals are worked directly onto the background fabric. Petal 7 is then added, followed by 8 and 9 (either side of 7) and, finally, 10 and 11 are added at the front, leaving space for a raised centre. This raised centre is worked over a piece of felt with French knots and then applied, adding more knots.

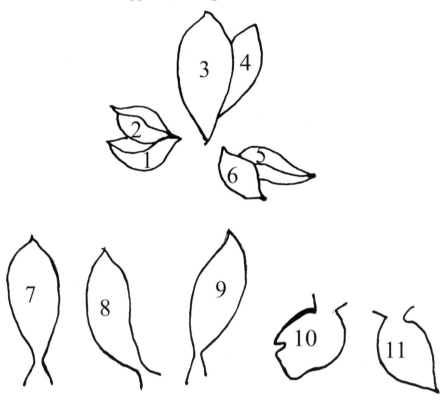

Grape Hyacinth

This flower was worked entirely in beads, using small white matt seed beads and pearl "tear drop" beads. The head of the flower was formed with a group of seed beads and then each pearl bead was added, with a seed bead at the lower end. Add a few straight stitches to indicate the stem.

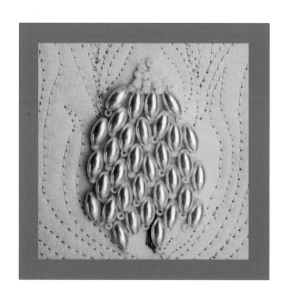

27

Daisy

The background to the daisy was worked straight onto the fabric, as shown in the diagram, stitching the petals and leaving the centre void. The raised petals were made using white cake wires in a similar way to the woven leaves described in the leaf section. Finally, two or three layers of felt make the raised centre - the top layer can be embroidered with French knots before it is added.

Large Iris Flower in Stumpwork

LARGE IRIS FLOWER

This flower can be embroidered by hand or, after the initial row of stitches, it can be machine embroidered.

Materials

10" square of background fabric silk, cotton, etc.
10" square of calico

Flower thread or other single thread such as perle, silk or coton a broder in the colour to be used for the outer edge of the petals - in the example pale mauve was used.

Threads for embroidering the flower: rayon, silk, stranded cotton, etc. You will need at least four shades of this colour - the example used from pale to deep mauve.

Small amounts of two greens, white, pale yellow and deeper yellow in similar embroidery threads.

Pelmet Vilene to the outer size of the mount to be used.

Cake wires no. 28 in white.

Fray Check (or other suitable product) to paint the edges of the petals to be cut out to avoid frayed edges.

Equipment

Fine embroidery needle

8" circular embroidery frame x 2

Small, sharp, pointed embroidery scissors

Petal 1 is worked directly on the background fabric, whereas petals 2, 3, 4, 5 and 6 are worked on a separate frame. The shaded area in the centre is padded with felt.

* These are the areas to be worked directly on the background fabric.   The middle* of the group of three in the bottom left corner is the stem of the flower and the rest are leaves.

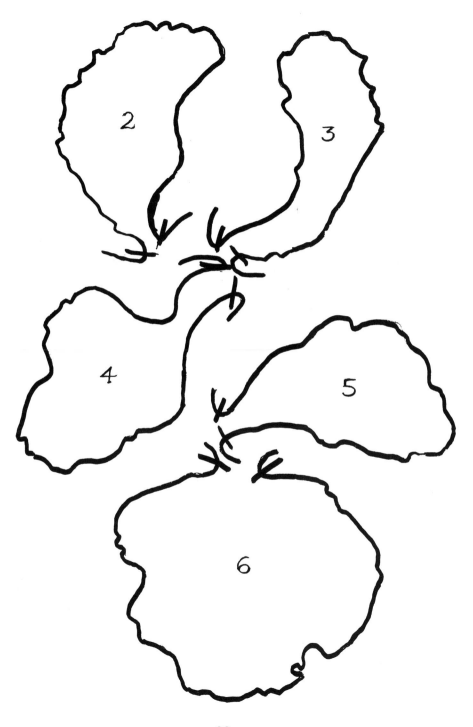

Preparation

Stretch the fabric tightly onto the frames one with the calico and one with the background fabric. For the latter, if a fine fabric is used, back it with a cotton square - refer to page 6 for instructions about this. Remember, the design must be placed on the straight of the grain.

Trace the petal shapes 2, 3, 4, 5 and 6 from previous page.

Embroidery

Mark the positions of the areas to be worked on the background fabric in pencil and outline with back stitch in the colour to be used to embroider them. The outer row of stitching will go over the backstitched edge. Work a row of long and short stitch all round the shape. Either continue to work in long and short stitch, shading the colours from light to dark on the petals, or machine stitch. Refer to the photograph of the finished embroidery for the placing of the colours.

Now, using the calico which is stretched on the second frame, mark petals 2, 3, 4, 5 and 6 with pencil. Couch the wires on, leaving about 1" loose at each end - these are to go through the fabric to secure the petals after they are cut out. Blanket stitch all round, over the wires, going down into the petal close to the wire and coming up on the outside again, close to the wire. (See diagram on page 10)

The first row of long and short stitch goes into the loop made outside the wire as shown in the diagram on page 86. This gives a good firm edge to the petal.

Continue to work in long and short stitch, shading the colours as in the worked example or embroider the rest of the petal using your machine. When the five petals are worked in this way, you can at this stage paint around the petal edges with Fraycheck to avoid frayed edges when the petals are cut. The small area shaded on the diagram must be worked as follows before petal 6 is cut out: trace the shape and cut out in felt as described on page 9, working the French knots on the top layer of felt before cutting it out.

34

Using a sharp pointed pair of scissors, cut each petal out carefully.
Position and secure in place, using the wire ends through the background
fabric and starting with petals 2 and 3, then petals 4 and 5 and finally
petal no. 6.   These can then be shaped by bending the wires to give an
attractive finish.

The completed iris could be mounted and put into a deep box frame or,
alternatively, set into a fabric covered box as the example in the
photograph shown below.

Fruit & Berries in Stumpwork

Fruit and berries often formed part of traditional stumpwork.   These
were used to decorate archways and trays.   Padding with felt is a way of
producing larger fruits; berries are often worked over wooden beads.

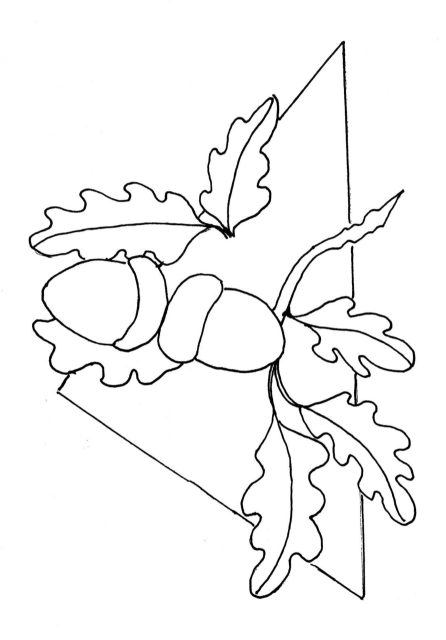

Acorns in Stumpwork

Materials

10" square of background fabric
10" square of cotton fabric (on which to work the raised leaves)
Small piece of felt
Stranded cotton in three shades of green
Stranded cotton in tan, red, orange, deep yellow and white
Single threads, such as flower thread, coton a broder, silk, etc., in acorn
 colours, fawn for the seed and brown for the cup
Pelmet Vilene
Cake wires, no. 28, in green

Equipment

8" circular embroidery frame
Embroidery needle
No. 24 tapestry needle
Tracing paper and pencil
Card mount

Preparation

Stretch the background fabric tightly onto the frame and trace the given
design onto it.   Trace the two acorn shapes and then draw four more
shapes, diminishing in size, for each acorn.

Embroidery

Cut out the smallest acorn shape in felt and attach this into the centre of
the space left for the acorn (see General Instructions on padding - page
9).   Continue working in this way until all five shapes have been
stitched into position.   Repeat for the second acorn.

Using the fawn coloured thread and satin stitch, and beginning to work
from the top to the lower edge in the centre of the acorn, work straight
stitches out to the side edge.   Then return to the centre and work out to
the other side edge.

Cut out a piece of felt the shape of the acorn cup and couch into place. With the brown single thread, work one long stitch from side to side at the top of the cup. Work a row of blanket stitches over this thread; at the far edge of the acorn, take the thread through to the back of the work and bring it up again at the beginning. From now on, work the blanket stitches into the loops made by the preceding row.

After two or three rows have been worked in this way, take the thread back up to the top of the acorn cup and couch the top row of blanket stitch to the top of the felt cup, ensuring that none of the felt shows.

Continue working rows of blanket stitch, gradually decreasing the number of stitches to fit the shape of the cup. Again, anchor the lower edge to hold the stitches in place over the felt.

Work the second acorn in the same way.

Draw the oak leaves to be worked onto the background fabric and, using two threads of the palest green stranded cotton, outline each of them in backstitch. The first row of long and short stitching in a single thread will go over this backstitching - this gives a good raised edge to the leaf.

Continue with the long and short stitching with the medium green thread, again using only one strand, and this time work from the centre vein into the preceding row of long and short stitch. Using a single strand of the darkest green, backstitch the central vein and then the side veins, noting that these do not meet each other when they reach the central vein.

Continue until all six leaves have been worked on the background fabric.

Lay out your threads in the following order: tan, red, orange, deep yellow, white and pale green.

Using two strands of the tan thread, work a first row of chain stitch around the outside of the marked triangle. Then proceed as follows:

Row 2 is worked in one strand of tan thread and one strand of red thread.
Row 3 - two strands of red
Row 4 - one red and one orange

Row 5 - two orange
Row 6 - one orange and one deep yellow
Row 7 - two deep yellow
Row 8 - one deep yellow and one white
Row 9 - two white
Row 10 - one white and one pale green
Row 11 - two pale green

Slip this piece of work from the embroidery frame and insert the piece of cotton fabric. Trace the outline of the raised leaves onto this fabric, wire, blanket stitch the edge and work the first row of long and short stitch going over the wire and into the loop of the blanket stitch edge. Continue to embroider the leaves as before.

At this stage, Fray Check (or a similar preparation) can be painted around the outside of the leaves, prior to cutting them out. Position each wired leaf, putting the wires through the fabric, bending them up behind the leaf and securing in place with a few stitches.

Put the original piece back onto the embroidery frame and back the work with a piece of pelmet Vilene ¼" larger all round than the intended mount. Using a thread to match the background fabric, back stitch in lines (see the photograph of the finished piece) inside the chain-stitched triangular frame and also outside the design.

Christmas Design in Stumpwork

CHRISTMAS DESIGN
with a poinsettia, holly and mistletoe

For the worked example, a piece of fabric with a poinsettia design was adapted. A complete flower was used as a background and then five separate petals were wired and cut out to be used as raised petals.

If a suitable printed fabric cannot be found, a piece of red fabric could be used for the background to the flower and petals with a little more embroidery added. It is not essential to work the whole area.

Another way would be to transfer the design to your background fabric and embroider the whole area.

This design shows the use of wooden beads as a foundation for the two types of berries.

<u>Materials</u>

12" square of background fabric (pale green was used in the example)
Small piece of printed fabric with a poinsettia design
Small square of green fabric (holly colour) to fit a small circular frame
Reel of Madeira No. 30 gold metallic thread
Stranded cotton in red
*A single thread, such as flower thread, coton a broder or silk:
      Pale green for mistletoe leaves
      White for mistletoe berries
      Red for holly berries
Gold beads for the centre of the poinsettia
3 wooden beads for mistletoe berries
3 slightly smaller wooden beads for holly berries
Cake wires, no. 28, in green
Bondaweb
A piece of Pelmet Vilene to the size of the finished piece of work + ¼" all round.

(*A single thread of stranded cotton could be used here but a slightly thicker thread would be far easier to use.)

Equipment

10" circular embroidery frame
Smaller circular frame to hold the fabric on which to work the holly
      leaves
No. 24 tapestry needle
Embroidery needle
Sharp scissors
Tracing paper and pencil
Fray Check and fine paint brush

Preparation

Stretch the background fabric tightly onto the 10" circular frame. Apply
Bondaweb to the back of a poinsettia flower and some leaves and iron
these to the background fabric. (See the instructions with the Bondaweb
for doing this as they may vary with different makes of the web-bonding
paper.)

Stretch a small piece of the patterned fabric onto the smaller circular
frame and select the leaves to be used for the holly. Here you could just
use a piece of green (holly-coloured) fabric and draw some holly-shaped
leaves on it. (The 10" frame with the background fabric on can be used
at a later stage for working the petals.)

Embroidery

Chain stitch around the edge of each petal and also around each leaf.
Add the gold beads for the centre of the poinsettia.

Slip the background fabric out of the frame and put in the patterned
fabric from which you need to select five poinsettia petals.

Wire these petals and blanket stitch around the edge with the gold thread,
using it doubled. With a single strand of red stranded-cotton, work a
row of long and short stitches into the loop of the blanket stitch as shown
on page 86.

Apply the Fray Check with a fine paint brush around each petal. Allow this to dry thoroughly and then cut out.

Position the cut-out petals on the flower background using the two wire ends. Stitch over the ends of the wire at the back of the work to secure them.

Work the three holly leaves, again wiring the edges (this time include a central vein), blanket stitching over the wired edge and working a single row of long and short stitch into the loops of the blanket stitch. Apply Fray Check and cut out as before.

The mistletoe leaves are worked using the needlelace technique - see the General Instructions for this on page 12.

Next work the berries. The slightly larger beads are used for the mistletoe berries: thread the tapestry needle with the white thread and bind around the bead, taking the thread up through the bead, over the outside and back up through the bead. Continue to do this until you have sufficient threads to go all round - there needs to be an odd number and room to pass the needle between them to do the needle weaving. Start to weave at the bottom of the bead and continue until it is covered and then take the thread back down through the centre of the bead. Work three berries in this way, leaving the thread end to attach them.

The beads for the holly berries are bound in this same way but this time the threads need to lie close together to cover the bead.

All the pieces are now ready to be assembled using the wires or threads to attach them. Bend the petals and leaves to obtain a natural look.

Place the piece of pelmet vilene behind the work and either back stitch in a thread matching the background fabric, as shown on the finished piece, or just attach by stitching round the outside edge.

The work is now ready to be laced over card prior to mounting.

Animals in Stumpwork

Animals are ideal subjects for stumpwork. Whichever way you decide to make the three-dimensional shape, you must always look carefully to see which part of the animal is nearest to you and which the furthest away.

Padding with felt

When this technique is used, the protruding areas need more layers of felt. The final layer usually covers most of the animal, thus covering the edges of the felt layers.

Trapunto padding

This is ideal for small animal pieces. The animals can be stitched on the background before adding a layer of cotton behind it and sewing through both fabrics just around the outside edge. You can then slit the backing fabric and push the wadding into the areas you wish to be raised. Always tease out the wadding well and add small pieces at a time. Sew up the slit to avoid the wadding coming out.

Stitching

Once you have decided which method to use, you next need to decide how you will stitch the animal. If you are padding with felt, you can stitch the animal before attaching each section. Once embroidered, you can add the layer by working more stitches over the edge of the felt, thus attaching it to the background fabric. (The camel was worked in this way.)

The stitching can be done by hand with long and short stitches or even using a sewing machine. (The elephant on the box lid was covered with needlelace - there are various stitches that can be used for this but this example used only rows of blanket stitch, each worked into the previous row.)

If you have a good-colour felt, this could be used unstitched, taking great care with stitching on the shape. Always complete all the shaping of the animal before you start to decorate it.

For the regalia to decorate the elephant or camel, you need scraps of fabric, ribbons, braids and some beads and some sequins could also be used - see the elephant in the photograph on the page opposite.

If you are familiar with beading techniques, bead hanging, as on the camel, can be used. If not, just sew beads onto ribbon to get a similar effect.

Elephant in Stumpwork

Elephant

Materials:

10" square of background fabric: cotton, silk or satin, etc.
Piece of grey felt, sufficient to cut out shapes 1-5
Threads:-   grey, single stranded thread for the elephant
                        (Coton a broder, flower thread, silk, etc.)
                    greens for the surrounds
                    bright colours for the ornamentation
                        (Including a length of gold or silver metallic
                        thread)
Narrow ribbon - scraps for decoration
Small beads and sequins for decoration
Small piece of Vilene and a piece of silk for the saddle cloth

Equipment

8" circular wooden embroidery frame
Sharp embroidery scissors
Tracing paper and pencil
Embroidery needle
No. 24 Tapestry needle

Preparation

Trace the shapes 1-5, the ear and the saddle cloth.   Cut out the
shapes and lay 1-5 onto the grey felt and cut out.

Stretch the background fabric tightly onto the embroidery frame.
Ensure that the straight of the fabric grain runs vertically, as this
will make stretching the final piece of work correctly much
easier.   Take the No 5 shape, lay it under the fabric and hold the
frame up to the light to get the position of the elephant onto the
fabric.   Lightly mark the leg positions with the pencil.

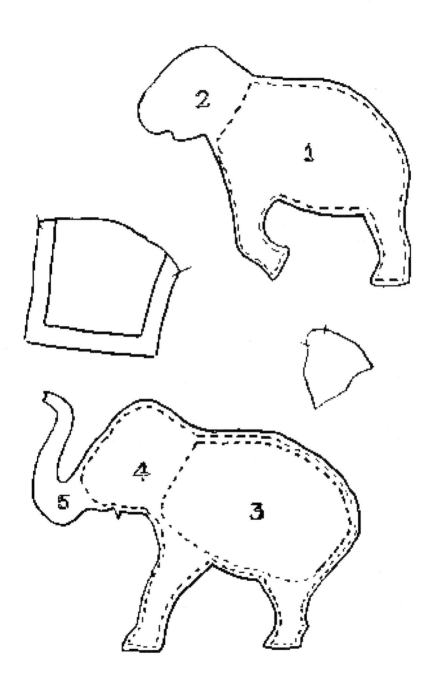

Use the pieces of felt in numerical order and stitch each in place as shown on the design sheet on the previous page. Stitch by coming up alongside the edge of the felt through the backing fabric and going down into the edge of the felt. The stitches should be about ¼" apart.

Embroidery

The padded shape is now ready to start the needlelace. Work the two legs furthest away from you first. Using the grey thread, begin by laying a thread at the top of the leg, then blanket stitch along it from side to side. The next row of blanket stitch goes into the loops made by the previous row. The stitching on these two legs needs to be smaller to suggest that they are further away.

There is no need to stitch underneath the saddle cloth, so mark the area to be covered by the cloth and stitch with a running stitch around this in grey thread. This line of stitching will be used to go into to hold the needlelace down, so make it about ¼" in from the edges of the cover as shown in the diagram.

Start with a straight stitch from A to B at the rump of the elephant to work into. The rows of stitches will get gradually longer as you work down. When you get to the lower edge of the saddle cloth, increase the line of stitching across from C to D. Continue until you have worked the other back leg.

Start again at the top of the trunk and work the trunk, head and right down the leg, keeping the direction as shown on the diagram. (You will sometimes have to add a part row of stitching to get the gradual change of direction.) Use a small bead for the eye - position carefully.

With a cream-coloured thread, work the elephant's toenails with satin stitch. Use tiny scraps of coloured ribbon for his bracelets. These can be attached by adding small beads.

Now decorate the saddle cloth. Cut out the shape in Vilene and cover with a piece of coloured silk. Edge the two sides and lower edge with ribbon and then decorate with stitching, beads and sequins as desired.

Add a small piece of ribbon across his brow and decorate with beads and an embroidered edging. Add a sequin on his cheek.

Work his tusk by laying several cream long stitches as shown in the diagram below and then satin stitching over them to make the pointed shape.

Add small tassels to the tusk. This can be achieved by laying a group of straight stitches which are pulled together at the top to make them look like a tassel or small tassels can be made and attached.

Work a loop of threads at the top of the saddle cloth and then button hole them together. Take a small piece of ribbon and fasten it at the top of his leg, get the correct length and neaten the top edge and, with a gold thread, fasten to the button-holed loop. Do the same on the other side.

Draw the ear on a small piece of Vilene and stitch with straight stitches from the top of the ear to the lower edge. Cut out and neaten the edges. Attach in position with a few stitches on the top edge only.

You are now ready to embroider the background as you wish. If you are a machine-embroiderer, you can of course do this on your machine. You might like to add some raised leaves, a palm tree or even an archway.

This is the elephant shown on the cover of the
booklet, illustrating different forms of
decoration.

Camel in Stumpwork

Camel in Stumpwork

This camel was worked on a decorated background using silk fabric in the centre and "colour through gold" stitching on congress cloth to surround it. A plain fabric could be used in the centre with a patterned fabric edge (as in log cabin patchwork). Rows of stitching on a plain border fabric would also give a lovely decorative edge. Here the instructions are just given for the stumpwork camel. The camel was stitched using flower thread. Other single strand threads can be used. (See the section on leaves, page 14, which lists other threads that are suitable.)

Materials

12" square of background fabric
Square of cotton fabric to mount the felt
Square of cotton fabric to mount the cover fabric
2 x 8" squares of felt
Oddments of fabric for the covers
Small quantities of beads, braid, ribbon and threads to decorate
Embroidery threads: camel colour (see paragraph above)
Sewing thread for couching shapes in place
Wadding - optional
Cake wires, no. 28

Equipment

2 x 10" circular wooden frames or a 12" rectangular wooden frame
Embroidery scissors
Embroidery needle
Beading needle
Tracing paper and pencil

Preparation

Stretch the fabric into the frame, making sure that when you start to stitch you work on the straight of the grain. Trace the shapes 1, 2a, 2b, 3 (the whole shape), 4, 5 and 6 (the cover).

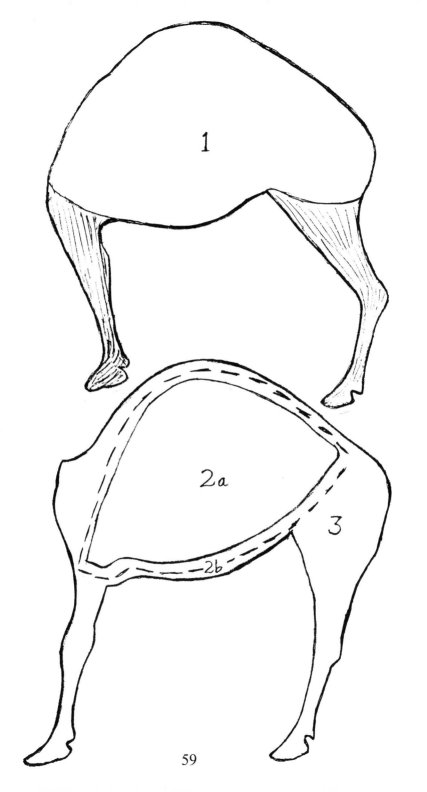

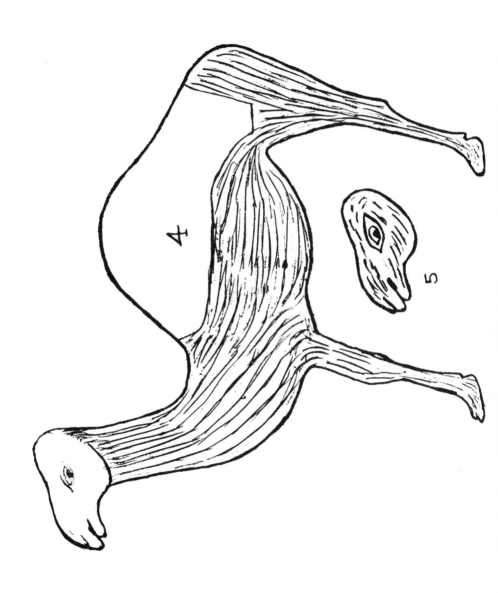

4

5

Cut out shapes 1 - 3 and place onto the first square of felt and cut out. Tack the second piece of felt on to a piece of cotton fabric that will fit your frame. Place the 4 and 5 tracing on to the second piece of felt and stitch around the area which will later be cut out.

Embroidery

Embroider the shaded area of shape no. 4 in a single camel colour thread, working the stitches in the direction shown in the diagram. Work the face with the details shown. Keep your stitching inside the stitched shape - more stitches will be added when the pieces are finally put onto the background.

Place the cut felt shape number 1 onto the frame holding the background fabric, making sure that it is correctly placed by laying the no. 4 tracing over it. Pay particular attention to the placing of the legs.

Using a single sewing thread, couch into place. It is best to come up through the background fabric and go over the felt edge. Now it is ready to be embroidered in the area shown in the diagram in the direction that is also indicated. Shapes 2a and 2b are used to pad out the body and can be stitched on in that order. As the camel has such rich regalia, it obviously belongs to a wealthy owner and is well fed, so at this stage between 2a and 2b you can add a small amount of wadding to make it even fatter!

Shape 3 gives the first felt layer of the two legs nearest to you and again adds to the body layers. Again check the position of the legs carefully.

Now the embroidered shapes Nos. 4 and 5 can be carefully cut out and added on using the embroidery thread and adding more stitches to the embroidery to attach them. Embroider the ears with straight stitches. For the tail, thread several thicknesses of your embroidery thread into a needle and run them through where it is to be attached, cut, plait and then tie a knot at the end.

The camel is now ready to be decorated and have the covers added.

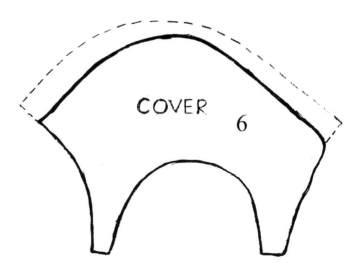

COVER 6

Stitch the patterned fabric to be used for the under cover onto the second piece of cotton fabric and stretch in the frame. All but the top edge are to be wired - lay the wire on the fabric (using the tracing as a guide), blanket stitch and then add a row of chain stitch (see page 9 for wiring shapes). Cut out close to the stitching around the wired edge, allowing a turning on the top edge (shown as a dotted line in the diagram). Fold under the top edge and stitch into place on the camel's back. Now add a short length of ribbon to make the 'tummy' band. Fold the cover down and keep in place with mock tassels - a group of straight stitches, which are then stitched over at the top to look like a tassel.

The beaded hangings are then added. (You could at this stage substitute braid or ribbon for beading, if you are not familiar with beading techniques.)

The centre of each hanging is worked first as follows:

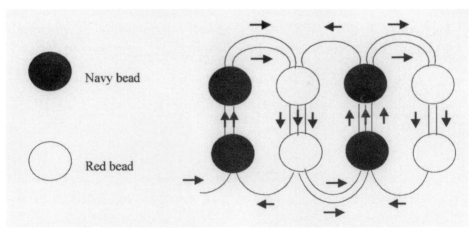

Using beading thread in a beading needle, thread two beads onto the needle and pull it through, leaving about six inches of thread hanging. Hold these beads firmly vertically between the finger and thumb of one hand. Pick up another set of two beads on the needle, pull the thread through the beads and fold the thread so that the two sets lay side by side between the fingers, Take the needle up through the first set again and down through the second set, as shown in the diagram above.

Repeat this procedure until there are 16 sets of beads. Then add a row of gold beads along each of the long edges by threading on a single bead and taking the needle up behind and over the thread between the beads of the previous row and then go back down through the seed bead and pull the thread firmly - see the diagram below:

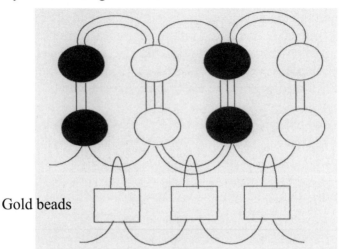

Gold beads

Make three groups of beads in accordance with the following diagram and add them to the bottom edge of the hanging.

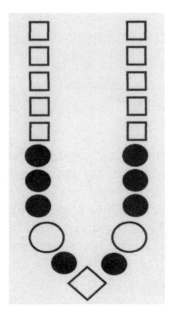

The 'garter' around each of the front legs is made as the centre of the hanging with small loops of five gold beads added.

The necklace is worked with the edging of navy and red beads as before, with loops of red, gold and red seed beads, plus a larger bead and then red, gold and red seed beads again.

The collar again uses the red and navy bead edging and this time a small gold ring is added before the collar is stitched on.

Thread a circle of five navy beads into the ring with a diamond shaped bead through which the thread goes when five navy beads plus one red bead are added. Take the thread back up through the navy beads, through the diamond bead and into a seed bead before returning through the diamond bead to add another spike of beads. Repeat this until you have five spikes in all.

At this stage the top cover is added. This is a rectangle of plain fabric, 4" x 2½". Fold over one long edge about ¾" and then tack the edge of the other three sides over. Decorate these three sides with a ribbon border. Now fold in the top corners:

Attach this shaped cover over the camel's hump and catch into place. Add a small tassel to each of the lower corners.

The harness is a length of narrow braid and should be looped over the saddle cover.

The camel is now complete. Do not forget to sign your work!

Lion in Stumpwork

Traditional 17th century stumpwork scenes are well known to contain certain elements. Animals were very likely to be included and often one was a lion. He usually sat on a mound which would be embroidered in rows of chain stitch.

Lion in Stumpwork

<u>Materials</u>
10" square of background fabric
Selection of threads in lion colours and greens - these could be stranded cotton, coton a broder, flower thread, silk, etc.
8" square of felt
Bead for an eye

<u>Equipment</u>
8" circular frame
Embroidery needle
Sharp embroidery scissors
Tracing paper and pencil

<u>Preparation</u>
Stretch the background fabric tightly onto the circular frame. Trace the whole outline of the lion and shapes 1, 2 and 3, as well as A, B, C and D. Cut out the tracings and then cut them all out in felt.

<u>Embroidery</u>

Stitch the whole outline onto your background fabric and embroider the shaded area in long and short stitch. See photograph for colours.

Stitch No. 1 centrally over the hindquarters of the lion, followed by Nos. 2 and 3 and then embroider.

Position A on the head area, stitch in position and then place B over the top. Embroider the shaded area. Then position C and embroider.

Finally add the face shape D and embroider the features, as shown in the photograph.

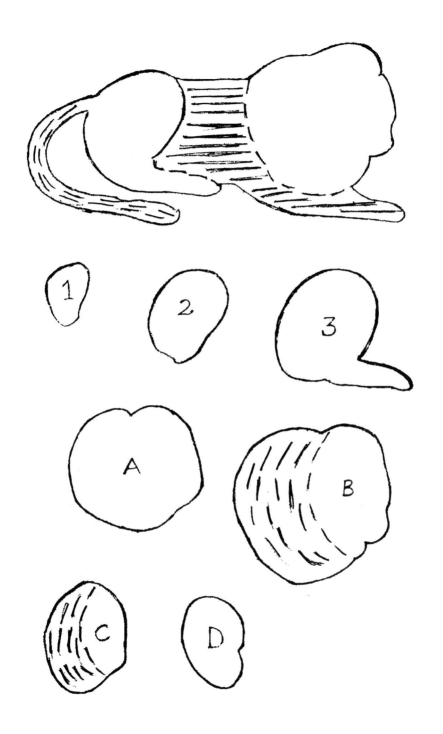

Birds and Insects in Stumpwork

Birds are excellent subjects for stumpwork. The bodies can be built up with layers of felt prior to embroidering the feathers, some of which can be added separately as an embellishment.

Traditional pieces of work often featured both peacocks and pheasants, as well as smaller birds sitting on branches.

Insects too were used and often these were
totally out of scale, e.g.
a snail might be the size of a lion's head.

Pheasant in Stumpwork

The worked example uses a background of dyed cotton to which salt has been added to give the mottled effect. A plain background could be used, which could then be embroidered later.

Materials

12" square of background fabric
12" square of natural colour cotton or calico
2 x 8" squares of felt
2 x 8" squares of firm sew-on Vilene
Pearsall's "Filoselle Embroidery Silk":-
       2 skeins Fawn 071
       1 skein each of the following:

Fawn	067	Cornflower	250
Fawn	069	Cornflower	251
Cream	087	Navy	276
Plum	090	Pomegranite	280
Green/Blue	188	Pomegranite	282
China Blue	209		
China Blue	210		

Cake wires, no. 28, in white

Equipment

Two 9" circular frames   Tracing paper and sharp pencil
6" circular frame   Embroidery scissors
Embroidery needle   Fray Check
A mount 8" x 10" with an oval aperture 7" x 5".

Preparation

Trace the shapes 1-7 and cut out shapes 1-5 in felt. Stretch one of the squares of felt and one of the squares of Vilene onto a 6" circular frame ready to work the wing shape (7). Stretch the background fabric onto one of the 9" circular frames. Attach the felt shapes 1-5, in numerical order, onto the background fabric, bringing the needle up by the edge of the shape and going down into the felt. (See the diagram of the complete pheasant for the positioning of the shapes.)

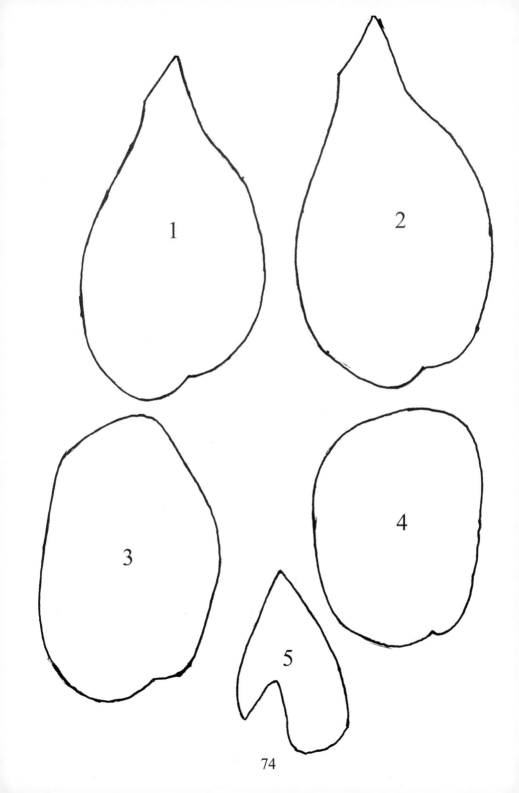

Embroidery

Using the 6" frame with the Vilene side uppermost, draw shape 6, which includes the head, and start the embroidery using one strand of the silk. With the Cream 087, embroider the beak; first go round the shape with a small backstitch and satin stitch the beak.

Backstitch round the eye area with Pomegranite 280, working two rows. Using the Navy 276, outline the actual eye. With Pomegranite 282, work tiny French knots to fill in the space between the outline and the eye. Work a French knot for the eye in Cream 087.

Starting with Green/Blue 188, work with straight stitches over the top of the head and round the back. Keep referring to the illustration to see the colours. Then start stitching below the eye with the Navy 276 thread and straight stitches. From now work in fans of blanket stitches, going through the colours as in the photograph - Cornflower 251 and Cornflower 250 on the left side and China Blue 210 and China Blue 209 down the right side of the head and neck. Work down in this way until you reach the first line (marked A).

The easiest way to work the next section, marked B, is to stitch the dark areas by working two blanket stitches side by side to form a triangle in Navy 276. Work all of these before starting with the other colours. For the lower neck area, work straight stitches in Fawn 069 around the triangles. Then fill in the remainder of the area with straight stitches in Fawn 071. Remove the work from the frame and put to one side.

Stretch the cotton fabric onto the second 9" circular frame and work on this frame, laying the wires as shown in the diagram to make the two long tail feathers. Couch on the wires, starting at the lower end, up to the pointed end and back down the other side in each case.

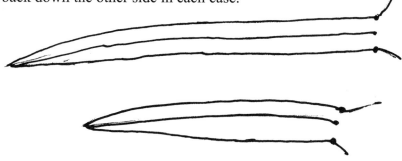

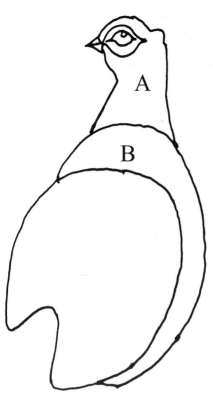

A

B

Shape 6

Blanket stitch, using the Fawn 071, over the wire and work the first row of long and short stitch using the same thread - see the paragraph on wiring a shape to be cut out in the section headed "General Instructions".

Next using Navy 276, work sloping stitches going up to the centre line. Fill in the spaces with Fawn 069. Finally, lay a further length of wire down the centre of the feather, oversewing with one thread of Cream 087 and one thread of Fawn 067. Fray Check around the edges and leave to dry. (Work the second tail feather in the same way.)

Using the 6" circular frame, stretch the second square of felt plus the Vilene onto it. Take the traced wing shape (7) and draw round it onto the Vilene.

Shape 7

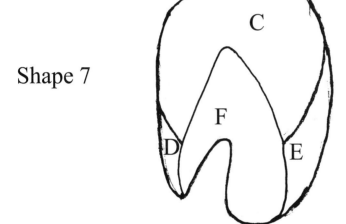

With a sharp pencil, in area C draw in the feather shapes, referring to the ones in the photograph. Outline the feather shapes in Plum 090 with chain stitch. At the centre top of each shape, work a detached chain upright in Navy 276 silk. Using Fawn 067, outline each of the detached chain stitches. Next, go round each one in Navy 276 back stitch. Fill in the remainder of each shape with Fawn 071.

The long wing feathers in areas D and E are worked in rows of chain stitches in Cream 087, Fawn 069 and Fawn 071. The top of shape F is worked with semi-circular rows of blanket stitch in Plum 090 and the spaces left are filled with straight stitches in Fawn 069. The remainder of the shape is worked in quite long straight stitches in Fawn 069. Work a row of chain stitches all round the shape in Fawn 071 and then cut out carefully close to this row of stitching and put to one side.

Working on the background fabric with the felt shapes already in position, start to assemble the pheasant. First, the embroidered section with the head is stitched over the felt shapes, starting with the edges of the head area and using Green/Blue 188 silk, stab stitch in place. Changing colour to Fawn 069, continue to stitch on this shape.

Next the tail feathers are added, pushing the wire through the felt and background fabric - a thick darning needle to make a hole is a great help!

Referring to the photograph below showing the leg and feet wires, bend a separate wire to represent each foot.

Wires for
legs

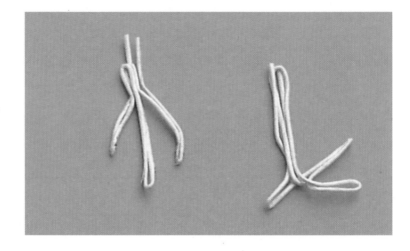

Using the Cream thread 087, closely oversew the wires in position adding a straight stitch at each end to represent the claws. Sew a single stitch in Fawn 069 at intervals down the leg and along each toe for the markings.

Now you are ready to add the wing area: holding the wing in position and using Fawn 071, work straight stitches coming up beside the shape and going down into the outer row of chain stitches.

At the base of section F of the wing, add more long straight stitches in Fawn 071 giving the effect of feathers over the tail area.

Finally, bend the tail feathers to give a natural look - a pleasant effect can be obtained by allowing these to extend beyond the edge of the mount - see the photograph of the finished and mounted piece.

Enlarged photograph of finished dragonfly

Dragonfly in Stumpwork

MATERIALS

5 peacock blue 9 mm bugle beads
2 seed beads to match
2 black seed beads (for eyes)
1 large oval bead - gold (approx. ¼" long) for the body
1 round gold bead for the head
Black beading thread
One square of crystal chiffon   )
One square of Vilene   ) to fit a small circular frame
Silver metallic thread

Equipment

A small circular frame   Sharp embroidery scissors
Fine wire   Tracing paper
Beading needle   Pencil
Embroidery needle

Preparation

Stretch the Vilene and chiffon together onto the frame.   The chiffon is to be the finished surface.

Trace or draw the two pairs of dragonfly wings shown overleaf.   Laying the tracing paper under the stretched fabric, hold up to the light and draw the wings onto the Vilene.

Embroidery

Couch the wire onto the wing shapes, beginning at the centre of the wings and ending there too.   Ensure that sufficient ends are left to cover the length of a pair of legs.   Each pair of wings is worked separately.

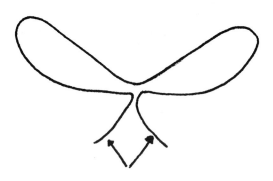

Top pair

These wires will be folded upwards under
the wings to form the second pair of legs

Lower pair

Using the silver metallic thread, blanket stitch around the wings and then
embroider them to suggest the wing veining - see the photograph.

Cut out carefully and put the two pairs of wings together and, with a
silver thread, bind the two together at the centre.

Using a single beading thread, go through the five bugle beads, through
the same colour seed beads and back up through the five bugle beads.
Then thread on the large oval bead followed by the 'head' bead.

Take the fine wire up through the bugle beads, the 'body' and 'head'
beads. Cut the lower end of the wire to about ½" and thread that
through the two seed beads and back up through the first bugle bead.

The spare wire at the head end is threaded through one black bead, which is then positioned on one side of the head, the wire is then taken back up through the 'head' bead and through the second eye and then taken back through the 'body' bead.

Cut a piece of wire about 1½" long and turn over the ends as shown below. This is then threaded through the wire holding the eyes in position. Using black beading thread, bind this wire.

Now, cut the two ends of wire on each pair of wings to give the desired length for the legs and fold over each end as before. Bind these with black beading thread. The pairs of wings are then joined to the body between the 'body' bead and the top bugle bead and finally the legs are shaped, bending as in the diagram.

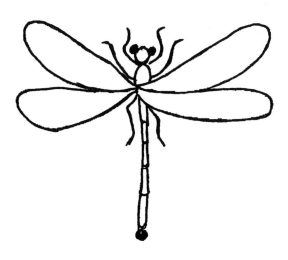

Butterfly in Stumpwork

This was an occasion when we used printed fabric.

A piece of butterfly fabric was stretched onto a small circular frame, a wire was couched in place around the outline of the butterfly and a row of stitching to fit in with the colouring of the printed design was worked.

Fray Check was carefully painted round the butterfly and, when dry, the butterfly was cut out and fastened in place by stitching the body and head and, finally, the eyes were added.

The ends of the wires were wrapped to form the feelers.

STITCHES

BLANKET

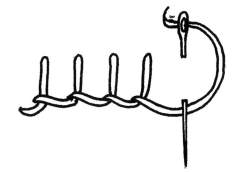

BLANKET OVER A WIRE

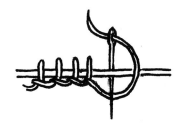

BLANKET DETACHED

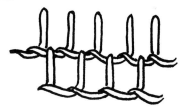

BLANKET FAN

BLANKET TRIANGLE

LONG AND SHORT STITCH

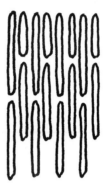

LONG & SHORT STITCH INTO BLANKET

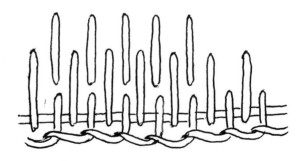

COUCHING

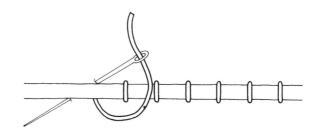

SATIN

CHAIN

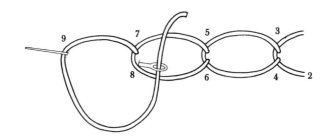

FRENCH KNOT

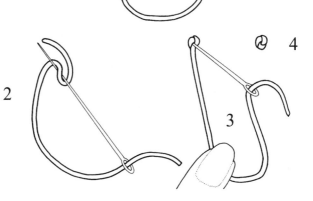

We find the use of raised embroidery for enhancing other techniques
sometimes more useful than making the whole piece
entirely in stumpwork.

Sunflowers

On these pages, just two ideas to give you some inspiration for further adventures in stumpwork. We see beyond panels of this three-dimensional embroidery to its use not only on the lid of a box (as on the opposite page) but why not inside the box itself? The miniature hand-embroidered garden shown above has been surrounded by six small mirrors (giving a kaleidoscope effect) and then set into the middle of a sunflower worked in French knots surrounded by woven petals, all contained within a deep hexagonal box, which has a lid for protection.

Another example of a poinsettia flower in stumpwork
set into a box with a divided top.

RECOMMENDED SUPPLIERS

Embroidery silks:

> Pearsall's
> Tancred Street
> TAUNTON, Somerset   TA1 1RY
>> Tel: 01823 274700
>> Fax: 01823 336824
>> Email: sales@pearsallsembroidery.com

> Madeira Threads UK Ltd.
> PO Box 16
> THIRSK
> North Yorkshire   YO7 3YX

Indian rayon threads:

> Fantasy Fabrics
> 42-44 Grant Street
> BURGHEAD, Morayshire   IV30 5TT
>> Tel: 01343 830600
>> Email: fantasyfabrics@talk21.com
>> Website: www.fantasyfabrics.ic24.net

Beads: Spangles
> 1 Casburn Lane
> BURWELL, Cambs. CB5 0ED
>> Tel/Fax: 01638 742024
>> Email: spangles@ntlworld.com

Cards: Brian & Chrissie Hall Cards
> 2 Hermitage Close
> WESTBURY, Shropshire   SY5 9QL
>> Tel: 01743 884113

ABOUT THE AUTHORS

Daphne and Jackie met through their mutual interest in embroidery and have been collaborating for the last six years, during which time they have written four books. They are both members of the Embroiderers' Guild and the National Federation of Womens' Institutes, for whom they also tutor.

After a career in teaching, mainly in Special Education, Daphne decided to take up embroidery seriously. She completed Part 1 of City & Guilds Embroidery and took a course on Goldwork at the Royal School of Needlework. Daphne now lectures and leads workshops all over the UK on many embroidery-related subjects.

Jackie arrived somewhat unexpectedly in the world of crafts after retiring from a professional career and moving to the country. She has taught hand-sewn fabric-covered box-making and calligraphy in Adult Education for many years and now lectures and tutors courses for many groups on a variety of subjects.

Daphne and Jackie exhibit, lecture and demonstrate together around Britain at international exhibitions and tutor courses in subjects related to their books. In 1999, they undertook a 6-week lecture and workshop tour around Florida at the invitation of the Sun Region of the Embroiderers' Guild of America, visiting 12 Chapters of the EGA.